THIS JOURNAL BELONGS TO A VERY SPECIAL PERSON!

Make this come to life with your colors!

Autograph here!

Pragya Tomar

Illustrated by Michela Fiori

Dedicated to my guru, Nanua-ji

Life is very simple.
What I give out
comes back to me.
Today I choose
to give love.
— Louise Hay

ISBN 978-1-952821-06-6 (Paperback)

https://www.PenMagicBooks.com

PenMagic Books provides special discounts when
purchased in larger volumes for premiums and promotional
purposes, as well as for fundraising and educational use.
Custom editions can also be created for special purposes.
In addition, supplemental teaching material can be
provided upon request.

Dear You,

My name is Pragya, and I wrote this activity journal for you. I want to share my life learnings with you as I believe I can help you grow into a confident, strong and wise young person. Having the right mindset and attitude can literally change your life. I wrote this journal with all my heart for my daughter, and she suggested I should share this with all the kids in the world. I want you to know I believe in you and want to help you explore and know yourself better so that you can lead a happy and fulfilling life.

With love and appreciation,

Pragya Tomar

THE KEY TO
BEING HAPPY
IS KNOWING YOU HAVE
THE POWER
TO CHOOSE WHAT
TO ACCEPT
AND WHAT
TO LET GO.

— Dodinsky

Fill this
with your
favorite colors!

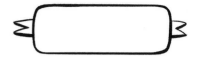

My real name is:

The name I wish I had:

Friends call me:

My parents call me:

Languages I know:

My best friend:

My birthday is:

My age is:

I was born in: (country)   (State)

I wish I was from:

My biggest secret:

My signature:

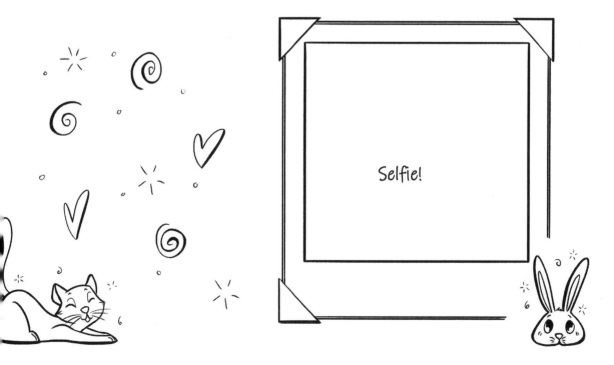

Selfie!

ABOUT YOU!

I am the ○ only ○ youngest ○ middle ○ oldest child

sketch yourself

My eye color is
- ○ green
- ○ blue
- ○ brown
- ○ black
- ○ other

My hair is
- ○ short
- ○ long
- ○ curly
- ○ straight

I am in grade____

I love to wear

Time I wake up:

Time I go to bed:

Top five words
that describe me:
- ○
- ○
- ○
- ○
- ○

I live with
- ○ both parents
- ○ one parent
- ○ grandparents
- ○ sibling
- ○ guardian

My pet's name:

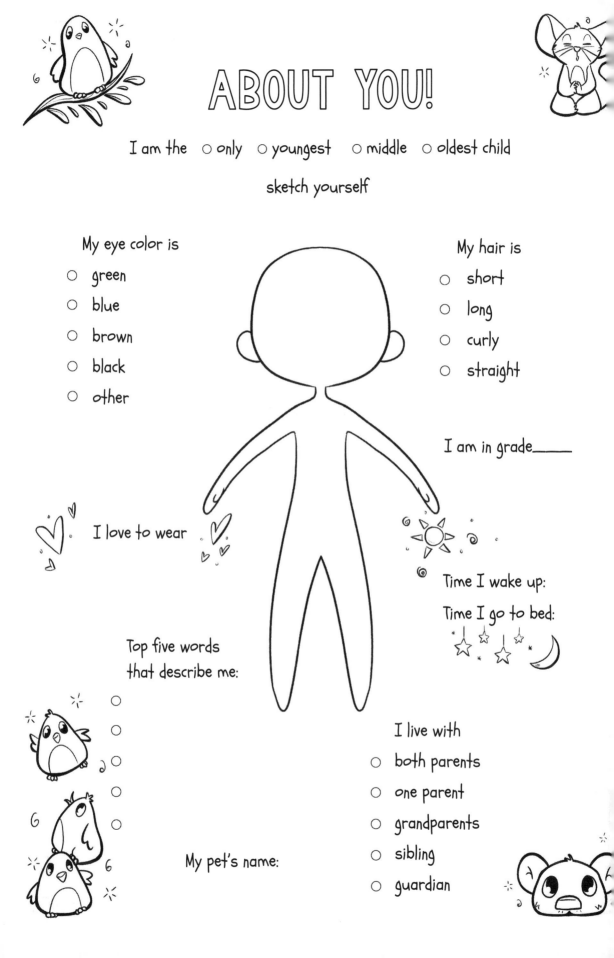

5 THINGS THAT I LIKE ABOUT MYSELF...

1)

2)

3)

4)

5)

MY FAVORITE

Season: _____

Movie: _____

TV show: _____

Book: _____

Store: _____

Ice-cream flavor: _____

School subject: _____

Game: _____

Month: _____

Food/snack: _____

Actor: _____

Actress: _____

Singer: _____

Fruit: _____

Pizza: _____

Outdoor activity: _____

Restaurant: _____

NOT SO FAVORITE

Season:

Movie:

TV show:

Book:

Store:

Ice-cream flavor:

School subject:

Game:

Month:

Food/snack:

Actor:

Actress:

Singer:

Fruit:

Pizza:

Outdoor Activity:

Restaurant:

color this

DEEP WITHIN EACH OF US IS A MAGICAL JEWEL THAT CANNOT BE SCRATCHED, IT IS THE SOURCE OF HEALING, JOY, AND WISDOM.

I AM A
MASTERPIECE

One in billions, yet I am unique.
I don't compare myself to others.

Dear You! You are a masterpiece. There is no one in the whole world like you. You are so beautiful, so loving, so kind, and so wonderfully unique. There are dreams and ideas inside of you that no one else has ever thought of and that the world so badly needs. Don't pretend to be anyone other than who you really are. You are powerful, beautiful, brilliant, and brave. You're my definition of perfect.

Don't forget – no one else sees the world the way you do, so no one else can tell the stories that you have to tell.

being kind

honest

respect

inspiring

helping others

friendly

What I am searching for is inside me.
My energy creates my reality.
What I focus on is what I will manifest.

TELL ME MORE

My favorite color is…

My favorite subject is…

I'm most happy when I…

My favorite movie is…

My favorite food is…

I really hate it when…

Yesterday, I…

Most people don't know that I…

If I won the lottery I'd…

Tomorrow, I will…

Right now, I feel very…

My favorite memory is…

Because you're alive,
anything is possible.
    -Thich Nhat Hanh

I AM ENOUGH

I am worthy. I deserve happiness.. I am loved!
I give and receive love freely.

Dear You! You have what it takes. You are strong enough, brave enough and capable enough. You are worthy. It's time to stop thinking otherwise and start believing in yourself . No one else has the dreams that you have. No one else sees the world exactly like you do, and no one else holds the same magic inside. It's time to start believing in the power of your dreams. Dear you, not next year, not next month, not tomorrow, but now. You are ready. You are enough.

HOW COOL IS THAT
THE SAME GOD WHO
CREATED OCEANS,
MOUNTAINS AND GALAXIES,
LOOKED AT YOU AND THOUGHT
THE WORLD NEEDED ONE
OF YOU TOO?

What you resist persists.

– Carl Jung

Because one believes in oneself, one doesn't try to convince others. Because one is content with oneself, one doesn't need others' approval.
Because one accepts oneself, the whole world accepts him or her.

– Lao Tzu

I BELIEVE IN MYSELF

I can. I will. I am limitless.

Dear You! Believing in yourself is the first secret of success. You are braver than you think, more talented than you know, and capable of more than you imagine. One of our greatest weaknesses is our lack of faith in ourselves. Be patient and kind with yourself. Never let opinions of others become the measure of your self-worth. Go confidently in the direction of your dreams! Live the life you want to live. Know that once you start believing in yourself, you will accomplish incredible things.. Without struggle, there is no progress.

"Believe in yourself and all that you are. Know that there is something inside you that is greater than any obstacle."
— Christian. D. Larson

Color each leaf of the tree.

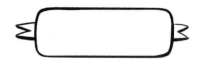

Write down goals you'd like to achieve in your life?
Be as specific as possible.

Wear gratitude like a cloak
and it will feed every corner
of your life.
– Rumi

Wake at dawn with a
winged heart and give thanks
for another day of LOVING.

– Khalil Gibran

I AM GRATEFUL

"Acknowledging the good that you already have in your life is the foundation for all abundance." – Eckhart Tolle

Dear you! Gratitude helps you fall in love with the life you already have. Life is so short, and we spend so much time sweating small stuff: worrying, comparing, wishing, wanting, and waiting for something bigger and better instead of focusing on all the simple blessings that surround us everyday. Take a step back, and look at all those great things you already have. Too often we underestimate the power of a touch, a smile, a kind word, a listening ear, an honest compliment, or the smallest act of caring. All of these have the potential to turn a life around. It's through the practice of gratitude that we discover happiness, peace, and contentment in our hearts and our lives.

Gratitude creates the most wonderful feeling. It can resolve disputes. It can strengthen friendships. And it makes us better human beings.

Things I am grateful for:

A strength of mine for which I'm grateful:

_____

Something money can't buy that I'm grateful for:

_____

Something that comforts me that I'm grateful for:

_____

Something that's funny for which I'm grateful for:

_____

Something in nature that I'm grateful:

_____

Something that changes, I'm grateful for:

_____

A memory I'm grateful for:

_____

A challenge I'm grateful for:

_____

Something beautiful that I'm grateful for:

_____

Things I love

Write and draw the things you love in the hearts below.

I love...

I love reading...

I love playing...

I love doing...

I love making...

I love eating...

I love watching...

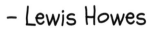

Feel the fear, process it,
and do what you need to achieve
what you've set out for yourself.

– Lewis Howes

I AM STRONG. I DREAM BIG. I DO MY BEST!

Magic happens when you do not give up, even though you want to. The universe often falls in love with a stubborn heart. –J.M.Storm

Dear you, please remember, nothing is permanent. You're not trapped. You have choices. Think of new ideas, make new plans, learn something new, imagine new thoughts, take new actions, meet new people, form new habits. All that matters is that you decide today and never look back.

Dear you! You've got this! Success is not built on success. It's built on failure. It's built on frustration. It's built on not giving up.

Try your best with no expectation and then let the universe take care of it.

Let's keep trying! Keep believing!.

Never give up.   Your day will come.

Every day is a new opportunity. Take a deep breath, smile, and start again.

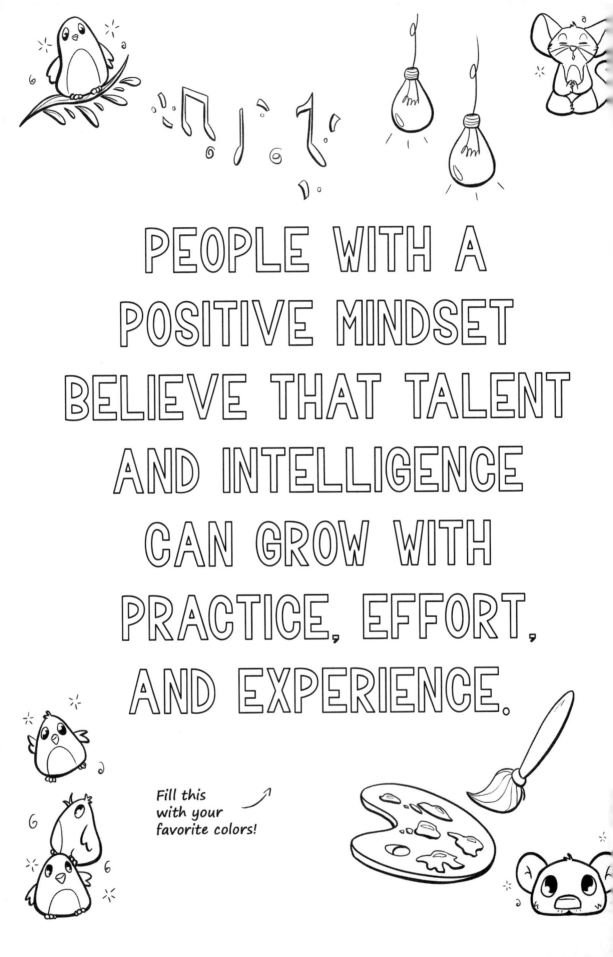

PEOPLE WITH A POSITIVE MINDSET BELIEVE THAT TALENT AND INTELLIGENCE CAN GROW WITH PRACTICE, EFFORT, AND EXPERIENCE.

Fill this with your favorite colors!

Can you color and say
these affirmations out loud?

What if
you could overcome
all obstacles and
scale any height...

What do you expect
to enjoy at the top?

I AM KIND TO MYSELF

The relationship with yourself sets the tone for every other relationship you have. – Jane Travis

Dear You! Treat yourself with kindness. The only one who gets to decide your worth is you. You, yourself, as much as anybody else in the entire universe, deserve your love and affection. So, start loving yourself compassionately and entirely. Be your own best friend. Encourage yourself, give yourself compliments, motivate yourself, and take good care of yourself. You're always with yourself, so you might as well enjoy the company.

Imagine the
little voice inside
you became bigger

What would
it say?

Imagine you had
a net to catch a
favorite moment
in your life

Which would it be?

MY FEAR TELLS ME:
I cannot succeed.

MY COURAGE TELLS ME:
I'm willing to try anyway.

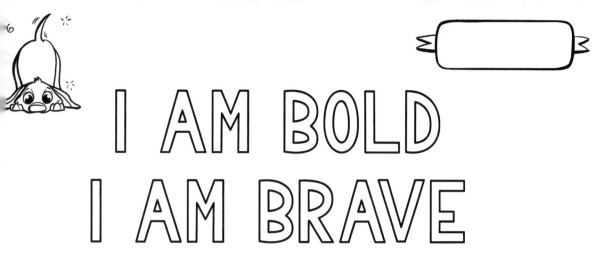

I AM BOLD
I AM BRAVE

Be bold enough to use your voice,
brave enough to listen to your heart,
and strong enough to live the life
you've always imagined.

Dear You! The greatest fear in the world comes from the opinions of others. A lion doesn't concern himself with the opinion of a sheep. The moment you are unafraid of the opinions of others, you are no longer a sheep. A great roar rises in your heart, the roar of freedom! Don't be scared to speak out.

Dear you, promise me you will not shrink yourself in order to make others feel comfortable. Don't base your self-esteem on other's opinions. Your actions will inspire others to dream more, learn more, do more, and become more. You are a leader!

To be beautiful means to be yourself.
You don't need to be accepted by others.
You need to accept yourself.

– Thich Nhat Hanh

I LOVE MYSELF

I love and accept myself unconditionally.
I am wonderful just the way I am.

"How you love yourself is how you teach
others to love you." – Rupi Kaur

Dear You! When you love yourself, your soul lights up! You
attract people who love, respect, and appreciate your energy.
Everything begins with how you feel about yourself. You
should eat like you love yourself. Move like you love yourself.
Speak like you love yourself. Act like you love yourself.
Loving yourself starts with respecting yourself, which starts
with thinking of yourself in encouraging ways. You, as much as
anybody else, deserve your love and kindness. Inspire yourself,
have faith in yourself, and love yourself. Never doubt who you
are. Spend time exploring who you are. In the end, the only
person you're ever going to truly live with is you.

Sometimes your mind plays tricks on you.
It can tell you you're no good, that it's all
hopeless. But remember this;
you are loved, and important and you bring
to this world things no one else can.
So hold on.

– Charlie Mackesy

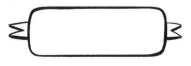

A man cannot be comfortable without his own approval.

– Mark Twain

THE UNIVERSE TAKES CARE OF ME

The whole universe is conspiring for your success. All you have to do now is simply trust. And the rest will come.

Dear You, when you are down to nothing, the universe is up to
something. If you don't currently see a positive sign, be patient,
the magic will happen. Your setback is setting you up for the biggest
comeback of your life. Remember, the universe has your back.
You are always supported, through thick and thin. Believe, change
is happening, even if you do not see it. Sometimes a NO or a rejection
could be the universe's way of protecting you from going towards
something that was not good enough for you. The universe sends
us exactly what we are ready for at the exact time we need it.
The moment you embrace your peace within and surrender the
outcome is the moment that the universe can truly get to work.

Remember this ...

It's okay to ask for help.

You are allowed to say no.

You are what you choose to be.

Anything is possible.

Follow your heart.

You are important and you matter.

Connect with the universe.

Believe in yourself.

Your mistakes don't define you.

You are worthy of great things.

You are so loved.

Feel Grateful.

You are enough.

Be authentic.

You can overcome challenges.

Be inspired by the success of others.

You can't stop the waves, but you can learn to surf.

I AM AWARE OF MY FEELINGS

Dear You! Emotional self-awareness is the ability to identify and understand your feelings and how they affect your behavior. Sensations and feelings are like waves in the ocean. Some come crashing in, while others roll in gently, but they always come and go. We can't stop the waves from coming, but we can be aware of their presence so they don't knock us over. Inner peace begins the moment you choose not to allow anything outside of you to disrupt your emotions.

Try accepting your feelings without judgment.

Please remind yourself, you are not your emotions. Say this to yourself, silently or (when possible) aloud: "I can handle this emotion. I am strong and able to handle this wisely, easily, calmly."

We have eight basic emotions. There is a purpose for each one.

Anger
To fight against problems

Fear
To protect us from danger

Anticipation
To look forward and plan

Surprise
To make us focus in new situations

Joy
To remind us what's important

Sadness
To connect us with those we love

Trust
To connect us with people who can help

Disgust
To reject what is unhealthy

All my FEELINGS

Share examples of when you've experienced these feelings!

A time I felt HAPPY was when

A time I felt ANGRY was when

A time I felt DISAPPOINTED was when

A time I felt NERVOUS was when

A time I felt EMBARRASSED was when

A time I felt CONFUSED was when

A time I felt SAD was when

MY FEELINGS

Fill colors to represent: often, sometimes, and never/hardly ever based on the key.

COLOR	I FEEL THIS WAY...
Blue	Often
Green	Sometimes
Yellow	Never/Hardly Ever

Confident

Responsible

Disappointed

Lonely

Worried

Anxious

Insecure

Shy

Happy

Unhappy

What do I know...

The stars will continue to shine.

I can always find my heart beat.

My breath is my constant companion.

Spring will always blossom.

Each day is a new opportunity.

Love never runs out.

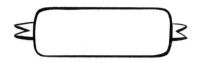

I AM CALM

I can manage my emotions in tough situations.

Dear You! When you can't control what's happening, challenge yourself to control the way you respond to what's happening. That's where your power lies.

I am confident I can deal with whatever rises.

Imagine you had the power to make someone very happy. For whom would you use this power?

What would you do?

What if with the snap of your fingers you could change yourself...
Who or what would you become?

NO WORRY JAR

A worry jar is helpful way to remove your anxious thoughts and worries. Putting your thoughts in the jar will help get them off your mind. What are some things that you'd like to stop worrying about for now? Write them in the jar below!

Every thought we think
is creating our future.

– Louise Hay

Send love to all
who cross your path.

I AM THE AUTHOR OF MY STORY

What if you had the power to write your own story?
The story of how your life will be. Would you do it?
Would you take charge of your story?

Dear You! You are the author of your own story. If you're stuck on the same page, remember at any moment you have the power to turn the page and start writing a new chapter. Your life is a book in progress, and you are the author. Get rid of the things that don't belong. Add more of the things that bring you happiness. Dream big and start writing your new adventure. Find the characters that are meant to help you on your journey. Embrace the middle chapters that are full of excitement and possibility. Write your own story because you are the only one who can. Write it with passion, with love! Write a good one.

No one else can tell your story, so tell it yourself.
No one else can write your story, so write it yourself.

Tell the story of your family
Every family has a history.

pic or sketch of your family

My family consist of....

My Family Story

Write your story!

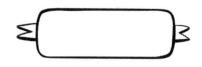

Write your story!

Every experience
is an opportunity
to awaken.

Be like a tree
and let the
dead leaves drop.

– Rumi

I FORGIVE.
FORGIVENESS IS AN
ACT OF SELF-LOVE

Dear You! It took me a great deal of time to realize what it meant
to forgive someone. I always contemplated how could I forgive
someone who hurt me. But after a lot of soul searching,
I realized that forgiveness is not about accepting or excusing
someone's behavior. It's about letting it go and preventing it from
disrupting your inner peace. Sometimes people hurt each other.
It happens to all of us. Purposely or accidentally, regretfully or not.
It's a part of what we are as people. The beauty is that we
have the ability to let go, heal and forgive.

IMAGINE
That you could forgive someone who hurt you.

How would your life change?

_____

_____

_____

_____

_____

_____

_____

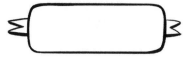

My Letter of Apology

Dear _____

I would like to apologize for _____

_____

This was wrong because _____

_____

I am sure it made you feel _____

Next time, I will make the better choice to _____

_____

I promise that from now on, I'll be kind and respectful at all times. I am sorry for my actions and I am glad you are my friend!

Sincerely,

_____

When stressed out or in doubt
look within.

You will never be able to escape from your heart.
So it is better to listen to what it has to say.
— Paulo Coehlo

I FOLLOW MY HEART

I trust the voice in my heart.

Dear You! If something excites you and scares you at the same time, it perhaps means you should do it. Have the courage to follow your heart and your instinct. Let your heart guide you when you're lost. Follow it wherever it may lead.

Listen to advice, but follow your heart and your dreams. Let no one tell you that they're silly or foolish. If something is important to you, pursue it. You deserve to be happy.

Try following your heart instead of your doubts and fears, and you will find the people and places that are truly meant for you.

What if
for once you
could reveal the
truth about how
you really feel.

What would
you learn?

Imagine
you could express
something in your
heart that you longed
to say but were afraid to.

What would that be?

Imagine
you could ask a bird
to deliver a special message...

What would it
say and to
whom would
you send it?

Imagine you
planted your
dreams.

What would
you hope
to grow?

Why are we stressing? Because we claim ownership to every thought and emotion that goes through us, we make them personal, instead of observing them without judgment and letting them go.

I LET GO OF THINGS THAT NO LONGER SERVE ME

When I let go of what I am, I become what I might be. – Lao Tzu

Dear You! Never spoil a good day by thinking about a bad day. You can spend your valuable time going over and over what could've happened or you could just choose to move on. Don't be afraid to walk away from things, places, and people that leave your soul heavy. Be mindful of where your thoughts are going. Stop replaying troubling memories. Stop worrying about the future.

Breathe. Be present. Then think of one happy thought that can make you feel better right here in this moment. Every new day we are born again. What we do today is what matters most. Starting today, you need to let go of what's gone, appreciate what still remains, and look forward to what's coming next. Life teaches us the art of letting go. When you have learned to let go, you will be joyful.
Give yourself time to:

Accept what is,

Let go of what was.

Have faith in what will be.

The fear of starting

I AM READY TO
TAKE THE FIRST STEP

"A journey of a thousand miles begins with a single step."
Lao Tzu

Dear You! To achieve anything in life, start where you are. The first step of your journey might be intimidating, but it's also full of excitement and opportunities. It is full of great promises and faith that whatever is meant to happen, will happen.

The secret of having it all is believing you already do. Take that first step in faith. Don't over think. Don't worry. You don't have to see the whole flight of steps. Just take the first step. The day you step outside of your comfort zone is the day your world will change. Have a dream and then take the first step! Affirmation: I intend to push fear aside and take that first step.

Rephrasing

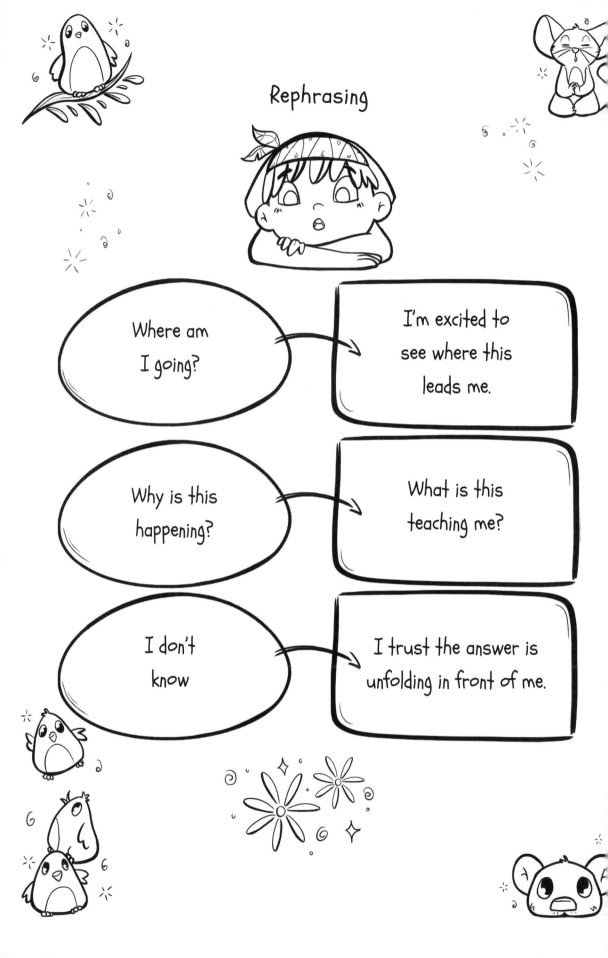

Where am I going? → I'm excited to see where this leads me.

Why is this happening? → What is this teaching me?

I don't know → I trust the answer is unfolding in front of me.

Growth happens when you...

ᗥ take risks,

ᗥ ask questions,

ᗥ help others,

ᗥ learn from mistakes,

ᗥ embrace change,

ᗥ are future driven,

ᗥ practice reflective thinking,

ᗥ get out of your comfort zone,

ᗥ feel affirmed and supported,

ᗥ are challenged to grow.

What is your dream job? What are five things you could do to turn your dream job into reality?

_____

_____

_____

_____

_____

_____

_____

Will you need to go to college for this career?

_____

_____

_____

_____

_____

_____

Do you know someone who has your dream job?

_____

_____

_____

_____

_____

_____

Can you research and find out what they did to achieve that?

_____

_____

_____

_____

_____

_____

_____

Give yourself permission
to have fun!

I CELEBRATE LIFE

I bring joy to this world!

Everyday of your life is a special occasion.
Cherish every moment!

Dear You! You are meant to fill life with all the wonderful things that fill your heart with joy. You are meant to live in a way that lights your soul from the inside out. Celebrate your big and little wins. Grow every day! Nourish yourself! Compliment others whenever you can. Make art. Life is meant to be lived. Take a deep breath of fresh air. Go for a walk under the open blue sky. Explore the wild – hug trees, watch the animals, enjoy the sunrise. Enjoy the small things life has to offer. Learn to appreciate quiet moments. Celebrate your health, your strength, your smile, your life.

Find your passion

What was your favorite thing
to do when you were smaller?

What is your dream?

What is your favorite topic
to talk about?

What do you enjoy doing so much
that you lose track of time?

If you had five minutes and the whole
world was forced to listen, what would you say?

6

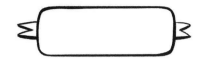

What would you do with your life
if you were guaranteed success?

What would you do with your life
if money wasn't an issue?

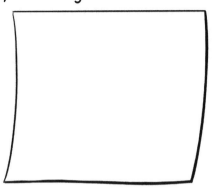

Whose life do you envy
the most and why?

What would you do with your life
if you had no fear?

What is your favorite subject
that you may pursue as a career one day?

Watch your thoughts like raindrops.

I AM MINDFUL

I breathe deeply. I enjoy every moment.

Dear You! Mindfulness is being aware, living in the moment, focusing on breathing, and paying attention to your thoughts as they emerge. Our life is shaped by our mind, for we become what we choose to think. Your mind will believe everything you tell it. Feed your mind with good thoughts. Feed it with truth. Feed it with care. Some days stink. Not everything is going to be how you want it. You'll get upset. But you can manage this feeling. You can slow down, take a few deep breaths, and pay attention to your feelings.

Dear you, you need to know that whatever you are feeling is okay. Listen to your body. Notice the sensations you are having. Pay attention to your mind talking. Are the words supportive and understanding ? Are you being gentle to yourself? Let your breath be infused with gratefulness. Be thankful that you can breathe, eat, walk, focus, ask questions, and meditate. This is how we practice mindfulness.

Aspects of mindfulness practice

Fill this page with your favorite colors.

Your mind puts
conditions
on your happiness.
It doesn't want you
to be happy now.
It wants you
to be happy when...

I LIVE IN THE PRESENT

I live in the moment. I am aware. I am one.

Dear You! If our minds hold thoughts about the past or future, we are not truly loving the present. Stay here, be present in this moment. Replaying broken memories causes anger and distress. Worrying about the future creates anxiety. Practice staying in the present. It will heal you. Living in the present is how you can live your life peacefully.

Enjoy where you are now. You are supposed to be right where you are. We are guilty of dwelling on negative thoughts about our lives. We get trapped into "where should we be" and all that does is cause stress and anxiety. Stay here. Stay present. Love this moment. Love yourself as you are.

Let's try staying engaged in the now.

Breath by breath,

let go of the expectation,

fear, regret and frustration.

Let go of the need for

constant approval.

You don't need any of it. – Surya Das

Practicing Mindfulness

Color them as you experience them.

Take a digital break

Chase a butterfly

Have a picnic in the backyard

Pay attention to the nature sounds

Hug (for no reason)

Breathe deeply

Have a family group hug

Draw a rainbow

Read a favorite book

Hold hands jump around the kitchen

Listen to the birds

Smell a flower

Pick wild flowers

Smile

I CHOOSE MY THOUGHTS

I have the power to control my thoughts.

I am in charge of how I feel.

Dear You! Your happiness depends on the quality of your thoughts. Choose your thoughts wisely, for they are the energy that shapes your life. Imagine your mind is like a garden and your thoughts are the seeds. You get to choose what seeds you plant in it. You can choose to plant love, hope, and abundance, or you can plant the seeds of anxiety, fear, and jealousy.

We become what we give our time and attention to. When you fill your mind with thoughts of kindness, love, faith, hope, and joy, your reality will become all of these things. You will start to see love, hope and kindness in the world. You will begin to feel positive as you go about your day. You will notice more of the little joys of life. You've tried listening to your fears and doubts and they have never brought you happiness. It's time to start choosing love. It's time to start believing in yourself. Learn how to choose your thoughts the way you choose your clothes every day.

Instead of:	Try:
I'm a mess!	I am human.
I'm a failure.	I'm learning.
Why is this happening?	What is it teaching me?

FAIL CHART

Did you just fail at something?

- **NO**
  - Good job!
  - Just don't get over-confident now. It's not always this easy.

- **YES**
  - That's okay. What are you going to do now?
    - **Try again right away.**
      - Yeah you are!
    - **Cry and try again.**
      - That's okay! At least you're trying again!
    - **Give up and quit.**
      - What?! Why???
        - "Because I didn't want it that bad to begin with."
          - Are people relying on you?
            - **YES**
              - Then you shouldn't quit. Follow through with your commitment, and don't let them down.
            - **NO**
              - Well, It's your decision, but failing is a part of the path to success. Instead of quitting, see what happens when you try a few more times. You can do it!
        - "Because I don't like to fail."
          - Everybody fails. It is part of life and is essential to success. Try again. Trust me on this.
          - Let's give it a fresh start.

MY MISTAKES TEACH ME

Mistakes are proof that I am trying. I learn, I grow, I do better.

"Anyone who has never made mistakes has never tried anything new."
Albert Einstein

Dear You! You are allowed to make mistakes. You are allowed to fail. Problems are guidelines to show you the way! You are allowed to start over from scratch. You are allowed to change your mind. You are allowed to try over and over again. You are allowed to struggle. No path is ever a perfectly straight line. Your path will twist and turn in directions you never expected. Life will bring you unexpected highs and lows that make you stronger. You don't need to have it all figured out right now because you will get where you are meant to be in time. To give up is the easiest thing in the world to do. But, to persist when everyone would expect you to fall apart; that is true strength. Learn from every mistake, because every experience is there to teach you and shape who you are.

What to do when I make a mistake

G R O W T H

M I N D S E T

I can learn from
my mistake.

I can improve
by working hard.

I will never
give up.

I am determined
to do my best.

Self-reflection
will help me succeed.

I can overcome
challenges with effort.

I can train
my brain.

It's okay to make mistakes.

Think of a time in your life when you made a mistake.
What happened?

_____
_____
_____
_____
_____
_____

What did you do about it?

_____
_____
_____
_____
_____

What did you learn from your mistake?

_____
_____
_____
_____

Think of a time in your life when you made a mistake.
What happened?

_____
_____
_____
_____
_____
_____

What did you do about it?

_____
_____
_____
_____
_____
_____

What did you learn from your mistake?

_____
_____
_____
_____

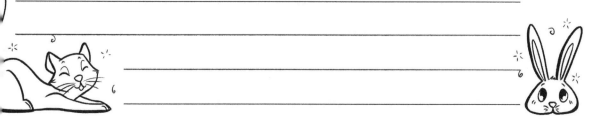

Be who you are and say what you feel
because those who mind don't matter
and those who matter don't mind.

– Dr Seuss

I AM AUTHENTIC

I am honest. I speak the truth.

Dear You! Authenticity is when you say and do things you actually believe. It is to know who you are and being brave enough to accept it and live it.

When you stop pretending to be anything other than who you truly are, and instead, put all of that energy into being yourself, your life will transform. You won't have to worry about fitting in, because you will be focused on simply being YOU! When you stop pretending to be anyone else, you will become your truest self and who you were meant to be. Authenticity is a practice – a conscious choice of how we choose to live. It's about being honest with your choice, the choice to let our true selves be seen.

Dear You! Try being authentic... be completely yourself so that everyone else feels safe to be themselves too.

Imagine
you could see deeply
into your heart

What do
you expect
you might
find?

Imagine you could give
the world some advice.

What advice would you give?

The words you speak become
the house you live in.
                    – Hafiz

Before you speak, let your words pass through three gates:
"Is it true?"
"Is it necessary?"
"Is it kind?"

MY WORDS HAVE POWER!
I USE THEM WISELY.

"When words are both true and kind they can change the world."
– Buddha

Dear You! Good words bring good feelings. Practicing silence is the best course of action when someone doesn't value your words. If speaking kindly to plants helps them grow, imagine what speaking kindly to humans can do.

Words can hurt or they can heal. They can break a heart, or mend it. They can hurt a soul, or free it. They can crush dreams, or enliven them. They can create boundaries, or melt them.

Words are powerful. Choose them wisely.

Tell me about a time when you used harsh words?
1. How did it make you feel?
2. How did you make it right?

_____
_____
_____
_____
_____
_____
_____
_____
_____
_____
_____
_____
_____
_____
_____
_____

KINDNESS BEGINS WITH ME

Ah. Kindness. What a simple way to tell another struggling soul that there is love to be found in this world. – A. A. Malee

Dear You! Be the one who makes others feel included. You never know what someone is going through. Be kind always. "People may forget what you said. People may forget what you did. But people will not forget how you made them feel." – Maya Angelou

A kind hug, a smile or a few nice words can help a person more than you think. Your kindness can turn someone's life around. Be kind to your family, friends, and even strangers. You never know how much someone needed that long hug or listening ear. Be known for your com-passion. Every deed of kindness grows the spirit and lights up the soul. Too often we undervalue the power of a hug, a smile, a kind word, a listening ear, or the smallest act of kindness. All of these have the promise to turn a life around.

Parents. and Kids trade places for a moment.
Can you put yourselves in each others' shoes?

PARENTS (or older family members)
fill in this side.

KIDS fill in this side

I think the toughest thing
about being a kid today is...

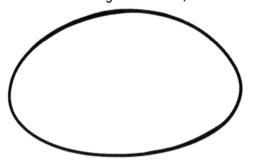

I think the toughest thing
about being a parent today is...

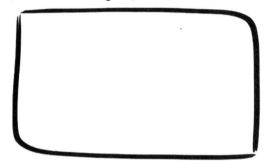

But the best thing about it is...

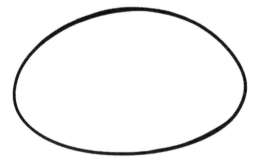

But the coolest thing about it is...

If I were a kid again for a day, I'd...

If I could be a parent for a day, I'd...

Carry out random acts of kindness.

Color them as you do them.

Leave someone a kind note

Give a compliment

Give a hug

Pick up litter

Write a thank you letter

Write a positive note to a classmate

Volunteer

Hold the door open for someone

Donate old books and toys

Do a chore for your sibling or Mom

Help someone having a tough day

Forgive someone for a mistake

THE GAME OF COMPARISON

GRASS IS GREENER ON MY SIDE TOO!

I am inspired by the success of others.

"When you are content to be simply yourself and don't compare or compete, you will find respect." – Lao Tzu

Dear You! Every minute you spend wishing you had someone else's life is a minute spent wasting yours. There will always be someone who has a little more than you, and there will always be someone who has less. Stop comparing. Start accepting where you are right now. Because you won't ever be happy if you don't learn to love your imperfect, everyday life. The only person you should try to beat is the person you were yesterday.

Dear You! Don't compare your journey with others. We are all walking our own unique path. Comparison kills creativity. There is room for you. Nobody has your voice, your experience, or your mind. Happiness is found when you stop comparing yourself to others.

IMAGINE that
a very wise person
shared with you
the secret
to having a good life.

What would she
or he say to you?

I am planting
this seed
for something I wish
to accomplish.
It is for...

Keep walking forward, no matter how closely your shadow follows behind you.

I AM PERSISTENT

A river cuts through a rock not because of its power,
but because of its persistence.

Many of life's failures are people who did not realize how close
they were to success when they gave up. – Thomas Edison

Dear You! Be that person who believes anything is possible and is willing
to work for it. You never know when you are minutes away from a
breakthrough.. That is why you keep going. That is why you keep trying.
That is why when you fall down, you get back up. Too many people quit
before even giving themselves a real chance. They stop because things
aren't happening fast enough or aren't working out how they planned.

Dear You, remember, some of the most important things in the world
have been accomplished by people who kept on trying when there
seemed to be no hope at all. All good things take time.
Be patient, and your time will come too.

Two types of confidence

My self value
comes from
the world.

My self value
comes from
within.

Confidence is not
"They will like me."

Confidence is
"I'll be fine if they don't."

I AM CONFIDENT

"I am confident because I can admit who I am, what I've done, and love myself for who I've become."

Dear You, the only one who gets to decide your worth is you. It doesn't come from the things you own or number of friends you have. It doesn't come from what someone else says you are worth. It's called self worth for a reason—it comes from you.

Your confidence comes from being youself and being proud of who you are. It comes from being someone that you can count on and someone you love. The outside things will change with time, but that won't change who you are deep inside—beautiful, limitless, wonderful, creative, strong, capable—and that is where your worth comes from.

IMAGINE
You could wave
a magic wand.

What would you wish for?

IMAGINE
You could be
your favorite
superhero.

What would you do?

Not all of us can do great things.
But we can do small things
with great love.
— Mother Teresa

I ENJOY MY JOURNEY!

Dear You! Don't wait for everything to be perfect. Accept and embrace where you are in your journey. Even if it's not where you want to be. There is a purpose to everything that happens in our lives. You don't have to know what comes next. You don't have to have everything figured out right this moment. You don't need to know your entire story.

You are a living, changing, growing soul, riding through your unique and beautiful journey of life. And that's exactly what it is— a journey— and it wouldn't be a journey if you knew everything that was coming next. It wouldn't be a journey if you knew how it would all turn out in the end. So be patient with yourself and smile at the unknown, because your story is just starting to be written.

IMAGINE

That you could speak to your favorite character from a book.

Whom would that be? What would you say?

List the places you wish to go!

By:

Connect –
Our influence reaches
further than we think.

I AM FRIENDLY

"I listen with my heart. I inspire those around me."

There are friends, there is family, and sometimes those friends become your family. Stick with friends who draw the magic out of you! There aren't many people that you just connect with. When you find those people, hold on tight to them.

Tell me more about your friends.

_____

_____

_____

_____

_____

_____

_____

_____

_____

_____

_____

_____

_____

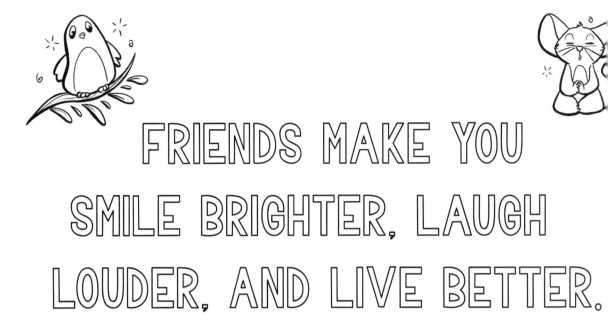

FRIENDS MAKE YOU SMILE BRIGHTER, LAUGH LOUDER, AND LIVE BETTER.

pic or sketch

Name: _____

We are friends because

Name: _____

We are friends because

Name: _____

We are friends because

Name: _____

We are friends because

Name: _____

We are friends because

Give negative thoughts
a hug and move on.

I CHOOSE POSITIVE THOUGHTS

Positive thoughts create hopeful feelings and attract positive life experiences. A positive mind looks for ways a task can be done; a negative mind looks for ways it can't be done. Being positive doesn't mean that everything is good – it's changing your mindset to see the good in everything.

Dear You, put your positive pants on; train your mind to see the good in everything. Positivity is a choice. The happiness of your life depends on the quality of your positive thoughts. When you focus on the good, the good increases. A great day that starts with a positive thought invites encouraging events throughout the day. Cultivating positive thinking is not about expecting the best to happen, rather it is about accepting that whatever happens is for the best.

Positive Self-Talk

I felt good when...

I am proud of myself because...

I had fun when...

This makes me unique...

I like this about myself...

I found this interesting today...

I learned from this mistake...

I love my....

An accomplishment I made...

The best part of today was...

I feel strong when...

I am good at...

A calm mind is a
creative mind.

I AM CREATIVE

Creativity is intelligence having fun! – Albert Einstein

Dear You! Being creative is being yourself. Creativity is the natural extension of our enthusiasm. Try to think up new things every day! Be curious. Everything you don't know is something you can learn. Create music, play with colors, write a poem, create a sculpture! Being creative is seeing the same thing as everybody else but thinking of something different. Being creative is the essence of life! An essential aspect of creativity is not being afraid to fail.

Making something unique is an adventure!

Try creating!

Try creating something today!

Draw a picture of someone you love.

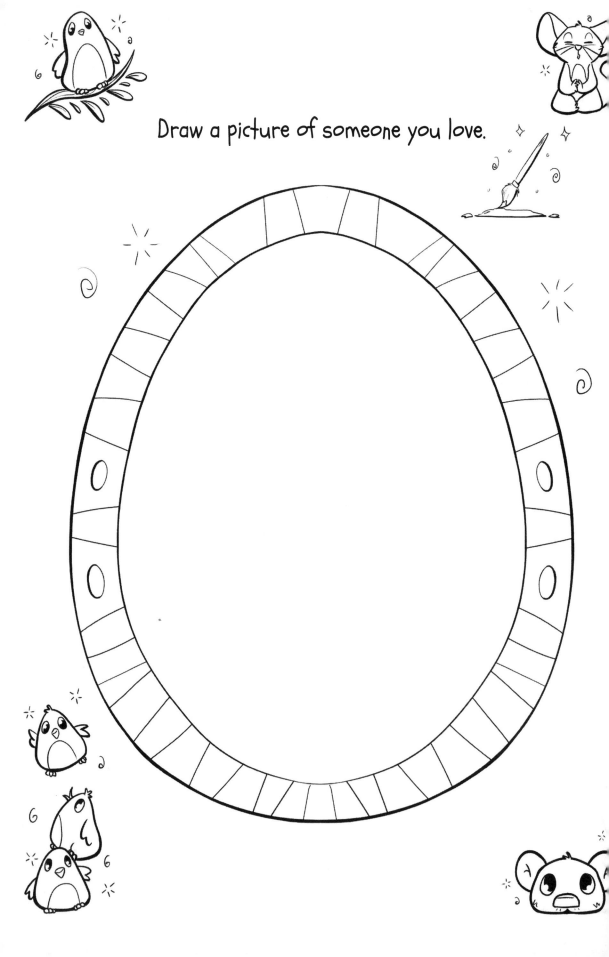

Create your
own sweet
wishes for
the people
you love.

What
would
they say?

All the elements for your happiness
are already here. There is no need to
run, strive, or struggle.
Just be.

– Thich Nhat Hanh

I AM WILD! I AM FREE!
I AM MYSELF!

To shine your brightest light is to be who you truly are.

– Roy T. Bennett

Dear You! You are unique. You have different talents and abilities.
You don't have to always follow in the footsteps of others. NO…
You are here to create your own vision and then bring that vision to
life. You are here to break away from normal, set new standards,
shake things up. You are here to be yourself and to be different. You
are here to live out your wildest dreams and create your own reality. You are here to follow your unique passions because what you
can do, nobody else can. To be original, just try being yourself, as
God has never made two people exactly alike.

Self-discovery questions

What are you passionate about?

What makes you happy to be alive?

How are you making the world a better place?

I wish I knew more about…

When I grow up, I want to…

Something I want to invent to make life better is…

Be the master of your mind. Self-discipline begins with the mastery of your thoughts. If you don't control what you think, you can't control what you do.

I AM STRONG !

Dear You, being strong can be a little hard, but anyone can do it. Being strong is to love unconditionally , to radiate happiness when we are unhappy, to forgive someone who doesnt deserve forgiveness, to stay calm in moments of despair, to show joy when you don't feel it, to smile when you want to cry, to make someone happy when your own heart is broken, to be silent when we feel like screaming, to comfort when we need to be comforted, and to have faith when sometimes we no longer believe.

I am strong because I've been weak.
I am fearless because I have been afraid.
I am wise because I have been foolish.

I am resilient like a river.
I can handle difficult things.
I am strong like a mountain.
I can manage through thick and thin.

My strengths and weaknesses

No one is perfect. We all have things we do well and things that aren't as easy for us. Highlight your strengths. Underline your weaknesses.

organization

making friends

being on time

making people laugh

eating healthy

reading

feeling confident

thinking positively

math

playing sports

listening to others

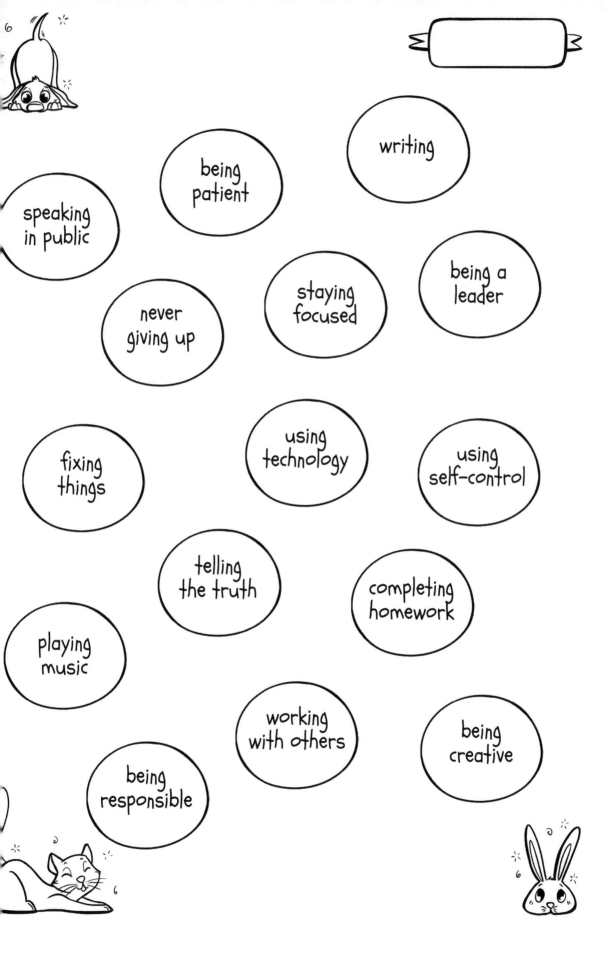

speaking in public

being patient

writing

never giving up

staying focused

being a leader

fixing things

using technology

using self-control

telling the truth

completing homework

playing music

working with others

being creative

being responsible

Fixed Mindset vs Growth Mindset

I'll never be able to do this.

I'll probably make mistakes.

I'm not good at anything.

It's not my strength.

People will laugh at me.

I can't be bothered trying.

It will be too much work.

I'll take a risk on this.

What strategy can I use?

I'll give it my best shot!

I can ask for help.

I can learn from my mistakes!

This will help me extend myself.

It's a great opportunity!

I GIVE UP!

LET'S DO THIS!

I BELIEVE IN THE POWER OF YET!

I have a growth mindset!

"I don't get it .... YET"

"I'm not good at this .... YET"

"I don't understand this......YET"

"This doesn't make sense .....YET"

"This doesn't work ....YET"

Dear You! Everything you don't know
is something you can learn!

It may not be easy, but it doesnt mean you're
never going to meet the challenge.

Things I'm trying to cultivate

I AM DISCIPLINED

Dear you, your mind is your instrument. Learn to be its leader, not it's follower. Self-discipline is the ability to make yourself do what you should do, when you should do it, whether you feel like it or not. The biggest challenge to self control is emotional regulation. Successful people know how to make their emotions their strength rather than weakness.

It's the ability to control oneself and one's conduct, for personal improvement. Self Discipline is needed to persist at difficult or unpleasant tasks until they are completed.

Let's talk about 11 habits of successful kids!

1. They live in a state of gratitude.

2. They have the power to control their mind and thoughts.

3. They educate themselves.

4. They make mistakes, learn from them, and move on.

5. They know the importance of self-care and health.

6. They know the importance of being independent.

7. They smile and laugh a lot.

8. They make goals and stick to them with hard work

   and perseverance.

9. They support their friends and enjoy their success.

10. They treat others with kindness.

11. They are authentic.

Dear You! Hope you enjoyed going through this journal and found some value in my suggestions.

If you would like to get in touch with me, please email me PenMagicBooks@gmail.com

With love and appreciation,
Pragya Tomar